Valleys and High Places

Walking with God

DEBORAH LOFTON

*The Lord gave the word: great
was the company of those that
published it.*

Psalm 68:11

*I dedicate my first book to my children and grandchildren in hopes that it will inspire you to follow your dreams. And always remember nothing is impossible, if you put God first.
I love you dearly.*

Table of Contents

Introduction

Is God pleased with my walk with Him?

It is a question that should be a part of our daily discussion with God. The question goes beyond the physical act of walking to encompass the mental and spiritual act of companionship with God. As we walk in the unity and fellowship of the spirit, we are to be pleasing to Him.

The purpose of the walk is to follow where He leads us.

Walking with God will eventually lead us to valleys, mountains, hills and high places as we grow in grace. Some walks will be pleasant, others challenging, maybe even dangerous (David). Some walks will become walks of faith through uncharted territories, leading the chosen through transformation to do greater works, still other walks become tests of faith to walk toward the edge and step out of the boat. The valley walk will be different from the mountain walk. But the goal remains the same-walk in the unity and fellowship of the spirit.

We must walk because God is motion.

No matter which verse of scripture we may choose to read, He (God) is moving, acting or performing. We are all familiar with God is, God shall, God can, God will and so on. To walk with God, to be with God or a part of Him requires constant action on our part; every commandment given to us requires action from us. Shall (shalt) is a verb used constantly by our Father and His Son. You shall love but you shall not kill as given to us in the Ten Commandments. We then must be in constant motion to remain connected to Him; listening, believing and trusting are actions essential to our walk. I (God) shall if you (the believer) will... and that keeps us in motion together.

Walk Through
the Valleys

One of the most frequently quoted passages of scripture is found in the book of Psalm number 23. Within those quoted verses is the mention of a walk through a valley that leads to a wealthy place of provision. David by his faith and self-encouragement received some assurances, while going through *the valley.*

> *Yea, though I walk through the valley of the shadow of death. I will fear no evil: for thou art with me; thy rod and thy staff they comfort me.*
>
> Psalm 23:4 (KJV)

David experienced the presence of God (*for thou art with me*) as he began the motion of walking; he received comfort, a prepared table, a new anointing and an overflow (*my cup runneth over*). New goodness (grace) and mercy was promised for the rest of his life, and an eternal place with God when his earthly house dissolves (*I will dwell in the house of the Lord forever*). Undoubtedly there are benefits attached to every successful walk through a valley experience when we humbly enter as sheep led by the "Good Shepherd".

If we live righteous as Job did, we often find ourselves in a valley of ultimate testing with the hedge removed. If we experience new levels of anointing as Elijah did, we often find ourselves challenged in a Mount Carmel valley surrounded by oppositions and unified enemies. When we are destined for a leadership role as Moses was, we often find ourselves at a Red Sea valley with only a rod and impossible odds. When we are blessed and highly favored as Abraham was, we often find ourselves challenged to leave familiar people and places to follow a promise through unfamiliar and uncharted valleys. When we seek to enlarge our territory as Jabez did, then we should be prepared to stand alone to enter a valley with little notoriety, hidden among genealogies of great men with only honorable mention of who we really are.

Most valley experiences are the result of our quest for heavenly favors. We tell God, "I want to go to another level, I need more anointing, more peace, more joy, more…" of everything. And He simply allows us to be led to an unpleasant valley, that we often call a "TEST". It may be filled with temptations and fears, tears and torment, the shadow of death, dry and uninhabited land, enemies that are larger and greater in number or other "devilish" challenges.

Through this book we will visit a few of the highly traveled spiritual valleys which lead us to hills, plateaus, or mountains called high places. The high places are our destination to the Glory of God, to a true place of worship, a place of adoration for our Jehovah, to be in the very presence of God. The benefit of reaching the high places is that we never return empty handed. There are rewards for the traveler who completes a journey through these valleys. By the end of this book, you will understand how to go through your valley to re-take your high place. Let us begin our journey through these valleys to the "high places".

1

The Valley of Eshcol

Have you ever received a prophetic word from the Lord, walked into the blessing and walked away from it because of fear? The human side of you took another look and decided, the giants are bigger than the grapes. You began to look at the promise from your human eyes and the vision turned from what God said to what you saw, thought and imagined. You basically called God a liar.

> *Behold, the Lord thy God hath set the land before thee: go up and possess it, as the Lord God of thy fathers hath said unto thee; fear not, neither be discouraged.*
>
> *And ye came near unto me every one of you, and said, We will send men before us, and they shall search us out*

the land, and bring us word again by what way we must go up, and into what cities we shall come.

And the saying pleased me well: and I took twelve men of you, one of a tribe:

*And they turned and went up into the mountain, and came unto the **valley of Eshcol,** and searched it out.*

And they took of the fruit of the land in their hands, and brought it down unto us, and brought us word again, and said, It is a good land which the Lord our God does give us.

Deuteronomy 1:21-25

When Moses appointed Joshua and Caleb along with ten others to spy out this valley of Eshcol, there were no maps or directions set forth by previous travelers on how to maneuver through this vast valley. The recognizance team was sent to gather information about the land God had promised to the children of Israel.

There were no confrontations or threats reported against the Israelite spies as they entered this valley. God allowed them to enter and taste of the fruits of the land, to walk on promised ground and pick unusual fruit from an unusual vineyard as evidence of the reality of the vision. The **valley of Eshcol** is filled with the visual manifestation of a promise. At this point while in the valley, all twelve spies agreed that this was a prosperous and productive place. God led them in at the time of the first fruits, when fruits were enticingly ripe and ready.

The mandate seems simple "Walk in by faith and possess it". The Israelites spies must have been excited, walking on a spiritually high cloud when they entered such a fruitful place as Eschol. There is a great supply of both food and water; natural and supernatural provisions are evident. The living conditions are excellent, it's a land of promise and there would be no lack or desire unfulfilled. While in this valley the believers walk in God's promises and taste of His goodness. They see the vision with clarity before reaching the end of the valley. For forty days, they gathered information and walked on promised ground. Never once does the scripture mention disagreement among the twelve while in the valley, walking in the blessing.

But remember as with all valleys, with all blessings, there will be challenges to the promise. It is not in the nature of Satan to stand by and congratulate God's chosen people on receiving this promise. But it is in his nature to challenge, abort, block or delay the pathway to the destined high place. By both mental and spiritually wicked devices, he plans their defeat in the **valley of Eshcol**, in their productive, fruitful place. Satan used visual distractions, Anak giants to disrupt the flow of God's plan. The Anak giants never threatened, confronted or even talked with the Israelites. Yet they became the decisive factor in the defeated retreat back into the wilderness.

Ten of the spies stepped blindly out of the blessing and vision of faith only to become consumed with fear and doubt. They became rebellious unbelievers who led others to miss the promise. They became a catalyst for a generation of losers, WHO SAW THE GRAPES BUT ONLY HEARD ABOUT THE GIANTS. The blessing is aborted at this time and they are left to wander away from the valley through the wilderness, so close to the Promised Land. An entire generation missed the promise because of what they heard.

For when they went up unto the valley of Eshcol, and saw the land they discouraged the heart of the children of Israel, that they should not go into the land which the Lord had given them.

Numbers 32:9 (KJV)

The men chosen for this expedition were selected by Moses from each of the tribes of Israel. Since leaving Egypt, this was perhaps one of the most important assignments of this journey. But the majority ruled, as Moses respected the wishes of the people and walked away from a promise. However, there are important facts to note about the character of the two positive visionaries or reporters who would one day return to this valley:

• Caleb was from the tribe of Judah, the "Praisers". This tribe went first into many tough situations, leading armies with no weapons, only praises. In difficult times they were called on to lead. They had a history of being victorious because they always praised their way through. They knew if they praised God, they could possess the land despite the giants. Their mentality was if God brought us to it, He can bring us through it if we only praise Him. They believed in praise before the victory; praise before entering the valley, while in the valley and when you come out of the valley. People who are true worship and praise minded, have positive attitudes in negative situations. Caleb saw the giants also, but those grapes were larger in his eyes and God had already promised them to His people. In spite of the giants, he praised God for the grapes.

• Joshua was a descendent of Ephraim, the second born son of Joseph. The name Ephraim means "God has caused me to be fruitful in the land of my affliction". Ephraim received the blessing of his grandfather that should have according to custom been given to his older brother. Joshua came from a blessed tribe which received inheritance by divine intervention. Joshua was the only spy that Moses called to stand before him prior to leaving the camp and gave him a name change. He changed his name from Oshea to Joshua, meaning Jehovah-Savior. Joshua was Moses' minister and assistant. He was from a tribe of Israel that were grandsons given a son's inheritance. They believed that no matter who the blessing should go to, God could turn things around and give it to whomever He pleased. Joshua was raised to believe that the wealth of the wicked could belong to the righteous.

This valley held promise(s), yet God allowed them to make the decision whether to enter and claim the blessing or to walk away and wait. They were basically saying "No deal" to God the first time. Many times we block our blessings by choosing to look at the negative aspects of the promise. We analyze with human vision, when the outcome is really spiritually generated and faith-based. Promised blessings have been abandoned by "what if's" since the Garden of Eden. The creation of doubt and mistrust in God's word is one of Satan's greatest weapons of defeat and vision mass destruction.

Imagine the disappointment for Joshua and Caleb when the Israelites walked back toward the wilderness, away from the valley. Not knowing that God had to remove some faithless people in order to keep His promise, Joshua and Caleb followed the crowd. This would be a time of purging and separation of the wheat and the tares. How often do we go through a season of shedding people and things that we consider losses, in order to enter our valley of Eschol? The second attempt to enter Eschol was no questions asked as Joshua took a "let's do this" attitude. He had seen the promise with his own eyes and heard the voice of God with his own ears. There was no hesitation to enter the same valley filled with the destiny of a chosen people. With victory this valley is the key that will unlock our treasures. It doesn't matter what occupies that hallowed space today, the fact is God wants you to have this valley. You suffered for it, you fasted for it, and you came through the storm, the rain, unfavorable conditions, fighting all the way to claim this valley. Enter in with praise and worship to the Great Jehovah, our Provider. This valley represents a Promise kept by God.

2

The Valley of Sorek

"Lead us not into temptation". Our Lord and Savior, Jesus Christ after fasting and consecrating for forty days was tempted. Have you ever been tempted? To take things that didn't belong to you, to tell a lie to get out of a sticky situation, to partake of forbidden things, or to reveal the secret of where your strength lies? The valley of Sorek holds the set-up for the Christian's down-fall, at the height of your anointing, at the close of a successful fast or at the beginning of your spiritual birth. There is no exemption from this valley. The moment the "sinner's prayer" is spoken; the challenge begins for the dedicated tempter, Satan himself, to bring defeat in this valley.

In this place, you don't have to look for trouble, trouble will find you. Walk the right path, become a true believer, honor God and His Son, be faithful to the Word of God and you will enter into

Sorek. This is a valley of choices and decisions for believers. There will be delicacies and delights, pleasing to all the natural senses. Curiosity and inquisitiveness peak at the moment of entry into the valley. The key to Satan's success is to use the vulnerability of quick decision-making to achieve his goal. The eyes, ears, nose and mouth are programmed to follow the directions from the mind (brain) through synaptic connections.

Therefore the attack must target the "mind" the rational part of man. Temptation starts here. A conversation between mind and spirit takes place; the pros and cons, what ifs and what about, the thoughts of past experiences and conversations of warnings all rehearse prior to entering the forbidden. The mind goes through a process of debates and ends with the final decision or outcome. Either walk away or indulge.

Eve literally "picked" but her bite was not Adam's bite. God's covenant partner, the first Adam made the ultimate decision in this valley and we know the outcome. Death was born and sin was shaped. Adam failed. But God provided man a second chance, a second Adam, Jesus Christ- the greatest survivor of temptations sting.

The latter temptation may lead to serious repercussions if given into the hands of your enemy. Satan would love to know the secret to your anointing, the one temptation that could possibly cause you to lose it; your Achilles heel.

Even though women have been at the forefront of many Biblical temptations, there was no greater than that of Judas Iscariot, the betrayer of Christ. The valley or Sorek, the valley of Temptation will always be a path for the anointed to pass through.

And it came to pass afterward, that he loved a woman in the valley of Sorek, whose name was Delilah.

And the lords of the Philistines came up to her, and said unto her, Entice him, and see wherein his great strength lieth, and by what means we may prevail against him, that we may bind him to afflict him: and we will give thee every one of us eleven pieces of silver.

And Delilah said to Samson, Tell me, I pray thee, wherein thy great strength lieth, and wherewith thou mightiest be bound to afflict thee.

And it came to pass, when she pressed him daily with her words, and urged him, so that his soul was vexed unto death;

That he told her all his heart, and said unto her, There hath not come a razor upon mine head; for I have been a Nazarite unto God from my mother's womb: if I be shaven, then my strength will go from me, and I become weak, and be like any other man.

And she made him sleep upon her knees; and she called for a man, and she caused him to shave off the locks of his head; and she began to afflict him, and his strength went from him.

Judges 16:4-5; 16 -17, 20

This valley was one of deception and manipulation by a woman named Delilah. A young man named Samson has left his own hometown to pursue the company of this well-known prostitute. He has been a unique person from birth, sharing the secret to his strength only with his closest confidants-his parents. He held the title of the strongest man to have ever lived. Besides being strong he was very clever and had a sense of humor. This painful journey through the valley of Sorek led to blindness, imprisonment, shame and death. Samson knew he had let God down by his decision to trust flesh. He was deceived by a woman to relinquish the secret of his strength.

Solomon fell into this trap when he turned his heart from God to serve idol gods in the high places. Adam ate of the forbidden tree in the Garden of Eden. David committed adultery and murder in his valley. We make choices in the valley to stand fast or fall into diver's temptations. When we take our eyes off God and see flesh, we stumble and sometimes fall. It seems that if we fall in this valley, we can never reclaim the same place.

David was not allowed to build the temple, we never heard any more great decisions made by Solomon, the wisest man to ever live and Samson chose death.

What have you given up in this valley? Have you given up your dreams, hopes, or a ministry, the writing of a book, your integrity, your favor, or eternal life? We can call this valley "Deal or No Deal with the Devil". We have choices in our Christian walk. Samson's strength was a gift that required abstinence and secrecy. The enemy knew that Samson was strong; they just didn't know the key to his strength. And they went to a lot of trouble seeking to discover and take this favor. He (Satan) often blindly sets up obstacles to hinder and to gain private information to kill and destroy your destiny. He seeks to extract that secret from the saintly and gifted to remove the favor of God. He doesn't have a clue where our strengths lie. As with Job, he (Satan) only knows that there's a hedge of protection that's not easily penetrated unless permitted by God.

That leads us to know that there are secrets between God and his anointed that the enemy doesn't understand. During our devotional time with God our worship and adoration sessions, Satan is not allowed to participate. He does not know what contractual agreement or covenant we have made with God in our prayer closet. Satan seeks to "get" into our psyche and send strong delusions to find where our deepest secrets to where our strengths lie.

The enemy is not allowed to know your secret, but God knows from early morning meetings and late night secret spiritual encounters that the anointed are faithful and trustworthy. The wicked spoiler has no clue except we fall into temptation and divulge our secret.

He doesn't know the strength but he understands the weakness of man. Notice how he sends a series of mishaps and troubles aimed at specifics. Finances, marriages, children, job related encounters, health and "church hurt" are the areas that get expected reactions from God's people. It often seems that these areas are targeted over and over again, that's Satan's secret. He's limited in what he is allowed to do to God's chosen. He uses different strategies on the same target; he takes things that he feels matter the most to us.

Job was an upright and perfect man; Satan knew of him and watched as this man grew in favor with God. But with bragging rights, it was God who suggested that Satan consider His servant Job. This wise servant realized that this testing was allowed because only God could remove the hedge of protection. But his understanding was not immediate, Job cried and grieved, felt betrayed and abandoned by God, but he came to himself. At some point the ashes came off, the burden of grief became lighter, he remembered the awesomeness of God, the strength of God, the unsearchable wisdom of God. Those things that were precious to him on earth really were not his to keep. ***"The Lord giveth and the Lord hath taken away"***. Bless the name of the Lord, the things that were taken were temporary and I did a good job taking care of them while they were in my possession. Job prayed continually for the souls of his children before trouble came, his cattle and herds were dedicated to God when things were well.

Instead of divulging secrets or cursing God, we should count it an honor that He trusts us to be tempted. But don't fall into these diverse temptations and give up the secret to success and favor. Job was tempted in this valley to curse God; his wife was used by Satan to make the offer of a way out of the pain. In essence she was used by Satan to say curse God and you'll feel better.

The enemy will never figure out our strength. He (the enemy) is allowed to try different theories that he and his demonic assistants have decided may be the key to the favor of God's anointed. But he has to test his theory. During Satanic board meetings, the brainstorming is unimaginable as the enemy attempts to figure out what will bring us down. Delilah used many faces and emotions to extract Samson's secret in this valley. After Jesus completed His forty day fast, the Board of Demons came up with a series of temptations to defeat his earthly assignment.

When we fast the devil will offer a free meal, irresistible aromas fill the air and invade our surroundings; every television commercial and billboard seems to be a food advertisement. A family member, who never bakes, may offer you a slice of homemade cake. When we pray the noise level increases, when we meditate the telephone rings and when we consecrate, distractions will come. Temptation can be as simple as ending a fast early to satisfy flesh and as complex as indulging in forbidden passions. We will learn more in later chapters about setting the atmosphere of worship, which involves lowering the ringer on the telephone and seeking God at an hour when the home environment is quiet.

Temptations await every believer in this valley. We all pass through this valley of temptation several times in our walk with God. In the beginning this valley was at creation, it involves choices, right or wrong, good or bad. Adam and Eve had choices in the valley (garden) of Eden. This was a perfect place to live; provisions were made available without work or toil. They could tiptoe through the tulips for real, barefoot. The temperature was perfect enough to walk naked without shame. There was no fear of ferocious animals or poisonous snakes. So why did God place something forbidden, edible and desirable in the middle of the pathway that Eve had to pass through? Whether Satan got into the serpent or the serpent was Satan, it doesn't matter but he showed up in the valley ready to tempt. He was there in the beginning with a purpose and succeeded using temptation to alter God's original plan for man's earthly existence.

When Jesus taught us to pray correctly, he included "lead us not into temptation deliver us from evil". Evil is ever present and we can so easily make the choice to sin, by losing focus.

3

The Valley of Elah

This valley will lead you to face your giants, the things in your life that are bigger than you, larger than you, things you fear and are unsure how to defeat in your life. The Hebrew word for giant is *Nephilim* meaning "violent" or "causing to fall". This valley holds things that seem to be unconquerable; doubts and fear have a tendency to lead to defeat in this place, causing us to fall from grace. It is here that we hear the voice of the giant but we don't go out to meet him, we pretend not to hear his taunts and challenges. Addiction is a giant; lust is a giant, jealousy, lying, envy, covetousness and so forth are giants to the human part of our being.

This is the valley in which David faced Goliath, the giant. This is a valley that we all go through at one time or another. The challenges here are meant to be violent against God's people and cause the elect to fall or fail. Giants are intimidating, larger than average, frightening and capable of defeating us mentally. These giants can be visible or invisible and may appear undefeatable.

In this season one of the most prevalent giants are economic hardships causing loss of jobs, foreclosed homes, and financial instability. This *Nephilim* has dared us to trust God during these times just as Goliath stood face to face with the Israelites with threats and challenges.

Facing our giants in this valley will be quite challenging. This is the challenge prior to reaching "destiny". David didn't look like a soldier or warrior but there was potential for success because of past encounters that went against the odds. The lion and bear prepared David mentally for this giant. He was confident, bold, unafraid, and visualized himself as a winner through God, with God's help and God's favor on his life. He knew himself and he knew God. Goliath was the first of many giants to challenge David; many more were to come after him both fleshly and spiritual.

The secret to David's valley success was not that he focused on the size of the giant, he was successful because he defended God's honor. The words spoken against God's people blinded David to the fact that this man was a giant. David probably began to reminisce on that day in the meadow when the bear threatened to carry off one of his lambs. It wasn't David's own life that he was concerned about, but there are times when we have to stand up for a principle. We have served faithfully with the few sheep, the five talents, the one coin, shared the two fish and five loaves in our lunch. All along building character and trust in God. The little things have prepared us to come to this valley. Times when we say "enough of this, I choose to fight", no matter how big this is, no matter how small I appear, I have the will to win and the determination to succeed. As children we could take everything the bully sent our way; except disrespecting mama, that's when something in us stirred and caused us to react differently. Something stirred in little David that day; the taunting of the enemy caused that dormant thing to awake. It was time to walk into destiny. But it took coming to this valley and facing a giant that set off his set up to move from the pasture to the palace.

David was sent to check on his brothers and bring word back to his father. He left home with specific instructions from his earthly father. But along the way, he transitioned into his heavenly Father's pre-ordained will. Instead of messenger, he became a "giant slayer", with a single shot to the forehead of Goliath. He teaches us to stand up for God in this valley; the battle is in the hand of the Lord, just stand up with boldness. The only thing David did was to except the challenge, pick five smooth stones, walk toward Goliath and swing by faith without hesitation. Shadrach, Meshach and

Abednego saw the flames, saw the men carrying them up fall down on fire but never felt any heat from the giant flames. Daniel walked among the hungry, giant lions without fear. Gideon faced a giant army.

We must conquer this valley of *Nephilim* in order to reach the high place to get to the real destiny. David approached this valley with no notoriety and no armor, no experience and no references, his only reference came from his own tale of bravery, his only weapon was a sling. According to God's purpose we enter unknown from the role of servant to our destined role as king and ruler over our giants.

David didn't leave the valley of Elah empty-handed; he carried the sword, the head of Goliath his enemy, blessed assurance, an added story to his treasures of triumph and the respect of a nation with him from the valley. Don't leave this valley empty as you go to the high place of worship. You deserve a prize when you defeat this valley foe. Take some more grace, mercy, more favor, and the respect of the angels in heaven when you leave. This experience will be helpful later when you return to this valley of Elah to face other giants; rest assured the things you bring out will assist with other challenges. You are not finished with your valley of giants, you will return with more experience and more understanding. *Nephilim's* stature and strength failed and did not accomplish the violence and defeat as intended with this valley trial.

What you bring from the valley will be instrumental in future battles. There are always spoils to be brought forth from the battlefield. Hold on to those things that you bring forth, you will need them again.

David carried Goliath's weapon (sword) from the valley of Elah and placed it in a safe place, in the hand of the priest, not knowing what he really had in his hand or the importance of this battle spoil. We find out later that David returned to get this sword to defeat another enemy. What did you bring from your battle?

Just as David received favor with God and man when he was in need of a weapon, so are we destined to receive.

> *And the priest said, The sword of Goliath the Philistine, whom thou slewest in the valley of Elah, behold, it is here wrapped in a cloth behind the ephod: if thou wilt take that, take it: for there is no other save that here. And David said, There is none like that; give it me.*
>
> *I Samuel 21:9 (KJV)*

Your weapon remains behind the "ephod" (a vestment (covering) or garment worn by the high priest in performing sacred duties) hidden behind the anointed covering, wrapped and disguised until your next battle. What you brought from the battle has been hidden, preserved and watched over in a sacred place. Waiting for your next battle.

4

The Valley of Dry Bones

The Valley of Dry Bones is not a place to be desired or a place to become a frequent visitor. This is a place of spiritual inadequacy, of loss and deprivation, lack of fluid, lack of life and activity, stagnant, spiritual death. As we will learn later in this chapter, spiritual death can be brought on by different circumstances, by suicide, assisted suicide or murder. How did you die? Who hindered you? All that's left in this valley are the bones, the dry bones. Can you live again?

No one wants to visit this valley of death, this graveyard of the soul to pay tribute to those lost. It is a lonely place, cold and gloomy with the misty fog of the aftermath of war and battle. This is an open burial ground, with no tombstones to rise above the dusty horizon, no colorful plants to adorn this place of rest.

These dry bones represent believers who have lost everything and have no hope; their very spiritual life has been taken away. Some were wounded in battle and unassisted they died, others were overcome by the blood loss and died; others were killed by friendly fire, whether mistaken for the enemy or killed by a careless comrade and some simply succumbed to the pressures of life, gave up and committed spiritual suicide.

We are killed all the day long by the mouths of our fellow Christians, who through acts of jealousy and envy destroy and assassinate with the tongue. That deadly evil member that lives inside each of us is filled with deadly poison. We communicate with friends in the church or family members the gossip we have heard or started, often from our own imagination. David's simple request was keep me from "presumptuous sins". How did you die? Or who did you murder?

Death By Friendly Fire

Many believers are killed by *friendly fire* from a member of their own team (church family, friend, or family). With no medical attention to the wound(s), they set up infection that can spread to other members of the body. The end results are death and finally slow deterioration in the Valley of Dry Bones.

This is one of the hardest deaths caused by acts of unforgiveness. Some of the greatest examples of forgiveness are found in the books of the Bible. Joseph provided a good example of forgiving others. His brothers sold him into slavery, gave him over to strangers and never returned to find out his fate. The Bible does not give an account of Joseph's thoughts, nor does it tell us if he pleaded with his brothers at the pit to rethink their decision. Did he plead or bargain with his captors or make known his father's notoriety or ancestry? The scriptures lead us to think that Joseph went peacefully, without a word. To those who truly trust God, going through a valley can be lonesome and fearful. But as a testament to faith in God, no matter how painful the journey or how many twists and turns must be encountered to the promise, we either persevere or die with a grudge.

Death By Backstabbing

Death caused by being stabbed in the back by someone you know or trust. This is a cowardly murder. This is an unseen adversary, someone trusted in your circle of friends. Someone you felt comfortable standing in front of, you thought they "had your back". Instead they killed your character, your spirit and you lie in the Valley of Dry Bones, lifeless.

Some of our greatest hurts come from fellow believers, family members and people who are in the same predicament. The hardest task for the believer is to look beyond the flesh and see the true enemy. It's easier to forgive flesh and blood when we are able to look beyond a face or the memory of the face we once trusted that now attacks from behind.

For we wrestle not against flesh and blood, but against principalities, against powers, against rulers of darkness of this world, against spiritual wickedness in high places.

Ephesians 6:12 (KJV)

Death By Lethal Injection

The depressed believer needs encouragement, counseling and prayer. They confide in the stronger members and even the pastor. What they spoke in confidence has been leaked to others who use it against them. Instead of prayerful intercession, the murderers use their confidants trust and mix scripture with gossip and sermons with speculation to inject the dose that kills. The lethal mixture enters the bloodstream and releases the poison. Whether guilty or innocent, death is imminent and the depressed believer's bones reside in the valley, very dry.

Death By Suicide

Self-inflicted bleeding wounds, hanging, and overdose represent the spirit of giving up, hopelessness, or self-punishment. You simply stop functioning, stop searching the scriptures, stop praying, stop fasting, and give up only to die spiritually. You're eaten from the inside out day by day by the uncontrollable issues of life. This is a self-destructive process that won't stop unless you come to yourself. This is how David must have felt at Ziglag, when he learned that his stuff, his family and fortunes had been stolen, as well as those of his soldiers who had been valiantly serving with him in battle. But he came to himself and encouraged himself before he committed any self-destructive act against his spirit man. He was overcome with grief but he shook himself and became an over-comer.

If these self-destructive thoughts are not dealt with immediately when they enter the mind, the believer will become suicidal and forsake life to become a skeleton scattered on the dry valley floor.

Death By Assisted Suicide

If looks could kill, sometimes they do in the form of assisted suicide. Those looks from someone else cause you to assume "there is something wrong with me". You assume that the person doing the critical looking is "holier than thou", but they really aren't. Their function is to throw you off with a facial expression and you will kill yourself with a complex. You begin to feel inferior and stop doing your good works. Spiritual high blood pressure, spiritual stroke and spiritual heart attack lead to spiritual death. The "haters" assist you with looks and words to literally kill yourself spiritually. You begin to see yourself through someone else's eyes, or view yourself by someone else's opinion. But "Who did hinder you?"

Accidental Death

Being in the wrong place at the wrong time can cause you to lose your life. When we place ourselves in a place of honor above God and take credit for things we had no control or hand in providing. We were gifted but used that gift for financial gain, become a prophet of lies, use our talents in the wrong way or even hide our talent and not use them as God intended. Our focus changed, something got our attention, many times becoming busier with other things and less busy with God's things. The prayer life suffered injury, the bible reading became less important, we were given caution lights and we failed to slow down until we became careless with the stop signs and red lights over time. .We became distracted along the way and as a result – accidental death.

Every now and then God sends an evangelist, a prophet or other anointed heroes to wake these dead bones and shake them back to life. It was Ezekiel, who was chosen for this task in the Bible. If we look at the character of Ezekiel, we can understand why God chose him for this duty.

Ezekiel was given a test question by God, "Can these bones live?" after being brought to this barren place, this Valley of Dry Bones. This was the question asked of Ezekiel by the all-knowing, all wise, God Almighty. He commanded Ezekiel to prophesy to lifeless skeletons, to dry bones picked clean by internal parasites, vultures, and other scavengers of this valley. Hopeless, wounded victims who once lived and functioned with blood running warm through veins and arteries supplying live tissue and muscles for movement. Lying lifeless and forgotten by everyone except God, who sent Ezekiel to stir up this valley, revive and restore.

The beauty of this valley is that you can triumph over the murder, the suicide and the other lethal devices. Come together bone to bone. Ezekiel heard a shaking in this quiet valley as the bones began to reunite. Rebuilt from the frame, the foundation was re-made and shaped by the hands of the master creator. Muscles, tendons and ligaments joined together, the skin returns to wrap and protect the internal framework. The flesh lay lifeless until Ezekiel commanded the wind to blow and the lungs expanded and inhaled and exhaled, the bloodstream was rejuvenated with oxygen that flowed to every part of the body.

What was cold now became warm, what was dead now became alive. The praise returned to the lips. When we entered this valley hope was lost until God sent someone to speak life. Often we are dead to the spirit, cold, and dry, scattered and lifeless. From this valley, our praise takes us to the high place of worship. Back to where God intended His creation to live in constant adoration and worship of Him. The Restoration process involves coming together of the total body frame on which to build, fusing to solidify the structure, muscles wrap the frame for support, blood vessel penetrate the muscles to carry oxygen and nutrients, and remove waste; nerves connect to conduct synaptic transfers to coordinate movement as they receive orders from the brain, functionality returns to this temple of flesh. The dry bones live again.

5

The Valley of Baca

Who passing through the valley of Baca make it a well; the rain also filleth the pools.

Psalm 84: 6 (KJV)

And now we enter our last valley, the Valley of Baca. A place you may have never heard of before now or you probably read the verse many times in your daily bible study, but simply read the verse and never stopped to meditate on its meaning. Like the prayer of Jabez hidden among verses of genealogies, this small verse is very powerful but may be missed to get to another highlighted, much quoted verse in Psalm 84, "no good thing will he withhold…"

The Valley of Baca is also known as the Valley of Tears or Weeping. Some scholars believe that Baca is located somewhere near Jerusalem; some say this is the valley you reach prior to entering Canaan, the Promised Land. Others believe it is Bakka, the Moslem Holy Land and some believe it's not really a place but a state of sorrow or pain that leads to Mt. Zion or Heaven, a place of peace and joy. It has been described as a dry place that is known for the balsam tree or bush which produces thorns that cause pain if they are touched by travelers through this valley.

The Valley of Baca is not a place to live but a place to pass through. We are all familiar with crying or weeping and shedding tears, whether crying ourselves or watching others cry. During disappointing times, loss of a loved one, joyful tears at weddings or the birth of a baby, some even laugh "so hard" until they cry. Whatever causes those salty droplets to fall from our eyes, we are all familiar with tears.

The Valley of Tears (Baca) is probably the busiest, most traveled, the most frequented valley of all the valleys mentioned in this powerful little book. This Valley probably gets the most nighttime travel of any valley, with the greatest breakthroughs coming in the morning hours before the break of day. There are millions who secretly travel through this valley; who cry behind closed doors with tears that are private, heard only by God. In the midnight hours pillows absorb the tears representing the pains and heartaches which are often undisclosed even to the person lying next to them. Tears are welcomed in this valley, this dry place; it was created to receive tears. They are relevant "attention getters" relegated by grace and mercy from the Valley of Baca to a final destination in heaven. Those salty droplets that leave our body in this valley somehow reach heaven and attract the attention of God and angels. God captures our tears and places them in a bottle and in His book; *they most certainly do have value in heaven*, they are as fragrant as the incense of burning tears that were offered during dedication and consecration with animals in the Old Testament. It's okay to cry. Our tears are stress relievers, they are the best anti-depressants not found in pill form.

> *Thou tellest my wanderings: put thou my tears into thy bottle: are they not in thy book? When I cry unto thee, then shall mine enemies turn back: this I know; for God is for me.*
>
> *Psalm 56:8,9 (KJV)*

One of the most touching stories of tears in scripture was when *"Jesus wept"* at the grave of Lazarus, his beloved friend. He actually delayed coming when He heard that Lazarus was sick unto death. He foreknew that a greater than healing miracle was about to take place. When He arrived there was much weeping by family and friends in their own Valley of Baca, their place of sorrow. He didn't answer any questions. He only wanted to know where he (Lazarus) was.

So why then did Jesus weep publicly at the burial site when He knew Lazarus would be raised from the dead? His entire brief ministry on earth was about one powerful word, "EXAMPLE". If Jesus showed emotions of joy, anger and sorrow and if He shed tears, in His own valley then we must conclude that tears have some type of significance in heaven. Because every facet of Christ's life from his conception to turning water into wine to walking on water to crying at a friend's grave was relevant. Every action conveyed a message of faith and hope and an example for us to follow. He showed us that crying is allowed.

> *When Jesus therefore saw her weeping, and the Jews also weeping which came with her, he (Jesus) groaned in the spirit, and was troubled.*
> *And said, **Where have ye laid him?** They said, Lord, come and see.*
> *Jesus wept.*
> *St. John 11:33-35 (KJV)*

One unknown writer says, "***The soul would have no rainbow had the eyes no tears***". Why are tears important both naturally and spiritually? What is the significance of tears in Baca?

One meaning of the word tear is *a drop of salty water coming from the eye.* It's interesting to note that the word "tear" also means *a small, hardened drop of the fragrant gum or resin of frankincense or myrrh, used in making perfume or burned as incense.* You are familiar with frankincense and myrrh from the story of Jesus birth when the maji, wise men presented these gifts to the newborn baby. In the Old Testament fragrant incense made with "tears" was used in prayer rituals to atone for the sins of man. Consecrated men of God, usually priests or Levites would offer an unblemished sacrifice to God along with the fragrant tears made especially for this most Holy Communion.

*Then the Lord said to Moses, "Take fragrant spices-gum resin, onycha and galbanum-and pure frankincense, all in equal amounts, and make a fragrant blend of incense, the work of a perfumer. It is to be **salted** and pure and sacred. Grind some of it to powder and place it in front of the Testimony in the Tent of Meeting, where I will meet with you. It shall be most **holy** to you. Do not make any incense with this formula for yourselves; consider it **holy to the Lord**. Whoever makes any like it to enjoy its fragrance must be cut off from his people.*

Exodus 30:34-38 (NIV)

During the Children of Israel's walk through the many emotional valleys on their way to the Promised Land, God gave Moses specific instructions for making the anointing oils and sweet smelling incense from tears.

Notice the word *salted*, salt was an important part of the purification and preservation process of this holy incense. We find a common ingredient to the incense (tears) made for worship and the tears God created that come from our eyes. *They both contain salt.*

The Bible in the New Testament tells of an uninvited guest who entered the home of a Pharisee and interrupted a dinner gathering. This guest, a bold, tearful woman with a repentant spirit, washed the Savior's feet with tears from her eyes and anointed them with fragrant oil from an alabaster box. Man looked at who the woman was, but Jesus looked into her heart and at the action performed in humility.

This woman was led through her tears of desperation and hopelessness in her search for directions, to bestow this random act of kindness upon the Master. Like many in the Valley of Baca, there are no words to describe the hunger and thirst for righteousness this woman must have felt. She cried. The salty tears flowed freely from this sinner's eyes upon the Savior's feet. Her hair was used to dry away the dusty wet mixture and she finally poured fragrant tears from a bottle. This was an expensive perfume, one of her most valued possessions; to be used for this special anointing, not on His head but to be poured on the lowest part of His body. She took the most humble seat, at the Master's feet. But the greater gift was hers to receive as she cried her way through this unknown valley, to forgiveness, to redemption and to honorable mention forever in the Word of God, the Holy Bible.

It doesn't matter if tears come from the eyes of sinners seeking for the right path or Christians going through trials and tests, the bottle in heaven doesn't discriminate. There are examples of many in the Bible, who cried and wept, even wailed in the spirit for both natural and spiritual direction, clarification, comfort, fulfillment and greater levels.

Hannah cried at the altar of the temple for a son, the man of God took notice and made intercession to the Father in heaven, a son was given to an otherwise barren womb. Like Hannah, in the valley of Baca, our barren wombs can become impregnated with a Samuel anointing, emptiness can be fulfilled, and a birthing of many things can come forth. Jeremiah was known as the "weeping prophet", crying for the sins of mankind, God took notice.

By morning those tears are replaced by joy, reassurance and lifting. By tears dead people are raised and live again; dead men begin walking. In the valley of Baca, tears are relevant. Tears go up before God like the sweet scent of frankincense and myrrh. There is no need to light a candle or burn incense; our tears have the aroma and essence of burning incense when they reach heaven. You will benefit from this Valley of Baca journey, its okay to CRY.

We learn to cry SPIRITUALLY in this valley. The repentant sinner often stands at the altar and the tears begin to flow without hesitation or prompts, they just flow freely down our cheeks. This is the emotional place in the Valley of Baca where promises are made to God and by God. When we are at the end of our rope and we go to God when we don't know what else to do, with that last tearful request for a solution, God opens His ears to listen. We have probably all heard the words "God was waiting patiently in line" for us to realize that He should have been the first course of action and not the last resort. But to come through to the high places and touch the heart of God Himself, the tears that come from our body become Holy and acceptable. They symbolize the defeat and brokenness that channels through this valley to the throne of God.

When Jesus was born in Bethlehem, the wise men came to worship him with gifts of gold, frankincense and myrrh. Tears are a sweet smell in the nostril of God. In the Old Testament, the offerings included incense and sweet spices purchased from a merchant. Tears from our eyes are an anointed fragrance that goes up before God and gets His attention. Jesus, our Intercessor in heaven, understands tears. When Lazarus, who was Jesus friend, died his sister Mary met Jesus and fell at His feet crying. If she wept at His feet, physically her salty tears most likely touched the skin of his feet. And like when the woman with the issue of blood touched his garment, something happened to the spiritual being of our Savior. Tears affect changes in heaven.

When Jesus began to weep, the atmosphere changed, forces in heaven began to activate processes to release a dead soul. Death was called before the Throne of God and given instructions to release Lazarus. Death does not take kindly to releasing souls back into living flesh. There was no discussion, such as when the rich man conversed with Abraham to send the poor man, Lazarus to his brothers. The Intercessor, the Son of God, the Prince of Peace, and the Only Begotten Son was crying and this required immediate action. No words were recorded to have been said by Jesus at that moment of weeping, but he prayed in St. John 11:41 ***Father, I thank thee that thou hast heard me.*** God heard him through his tears. Because tears speak to the compassionate heart of Jehovah, the answer was sure to be "yes".

Tears are symbolic, significant and have meaning in heaven. David was a known weeper, who frequently touched the heart of God with his tears. He found a formula that worked on the grace and mercy of heaven. David believed:

> *They that sow in tears shall reap in joy. He that goeth forth and weepeth, bearing precious seed, shall doubtless come again with rejoicing, bringing his sheaves with him. Psalm 126:5, 6 (KJV)*
>
> *Those who sow in tears will reap with songs of joy.*
>
> *He who goes out weeping, carrying seed to sow, will return with songs of joy, carrying sheaves with him.*
>
> *Psalm 126: 5, 6 (NIV)*

When Tabitha (Dorcas), a follower full of good works and alms deeds died, they called for Peter to come quickly to Joppa. Peter was surrounded in the upper chamber by women weeping and showing him garments this woman had made. Heaven saw the pain through the eyes of Peter and the atmosphere was affected. Before Peter prayed he sent everyone out of the room to change the atmosphere from one of mourning and wailing to an atmosphere of faith and believing. Heaven had already been set up for the transformation before Peter arrived; the tears brought Peter to Joppa. He only had to stand in the gap, return to the high place. I imagine the tears were on the hands and clothes of these widows, who touched Peter as he entered the upper room. He prayed as Jesus had prayed at the tomb of Lazarus, and he turned to the body and spoke, "Tabitha arise". By divine commandment, she opened her eyes and saw Peter. He brought her forth and presented her to the widows alive. Tears bring forth a fruitful presentation, whether healing, bills paid, resurrection of the dead, sight to blinded eyes or relief to a body racked with pain. Pure, sincere, dedicated and real uncompromised tears are anointed.

> *Then Eli answered and said, Go in peace: and the God of Israel grant thee thy petition that thou hast asked of him.*
>
> *And she said, Let thine handmaid find grace in thy sight. So the woman went her way, and did eat and her countenance was no more sad.*
>
> *I Samuel 1:17, 18 (KJV)*

Hannah "wept sore" as she petitioned God for a son. But it was Eli, the priest who interceded to affect the change. Weep, move to the high place and wait on the intercessor to take the petition before the heavenly Father.

Samuel, one of the greatest prophets to ever come forth was birthed by Hannah's tears. Ishmael, Abraham's son by a handmaid, was near death, when his mother Hagar, through her tears affected a change in heaven. Life is restored. Cry in this valley-Heaven is receiving your tears. This valley experience is not permanent.

Moving Up to the High Places

It is still God's will that man serve him in the high places. Most of us think of a high place as a mountain or rooftop meeting place, or we remember the scripture that lets us know spiritual wickedness is in high places. It would be wonderful to wake up early and be dedicated enough to walk outside our homes and go up the mountain to pray and worship our Jehovah. Since we are not all privileged enough to look out our windows and see an actual mountain, we must find a place within our limited environment to call our "High Place" of worship.

Whenever you leave a "valley" experience, there needs to be a mountain experience, a high place of pursuit for the presence of God. Victory is not silent, it is not quiet. Even when no words are spoken it manifests on the face of the victor in unspoken ways. The worshipper needs to immediately go into the overcoming, victorious praise mode of worship in higher elevation.

The "High Place" that you choose is to be consecrated, hallowed and private. It can be a closet, a living room floor, a bathroom, a small corner in the den, an attic, a balcony or an outside garden. It needs to be physically clean and free of debris, uncluttered and odor free. As private as possible, with little to no distractions, a "quiet" place that welcomes and invites your praise to saturate the atmosphere. This should be a place where you can cry in peace and listen undisturbed when God speaks to you. Family members should be aware of the sanctity of your place and leave you alone when you enter at your specific time. When you have established a "mountain, a High Place", the ground you have chosen now becomes Holy ground.

There are many hills and mountains that lead us to greater levels of anointing and blessings. We obtain benefits to compensate for "coming through" hardships and challenges, rewards for the forty days or twenty-one day hold-ups while in the valley (s). While in the valley we looked to the hills now wc arc walking in the hills, the high place.

"The greater the sacrifice the greater the anointing, the greater the anointing the greater the sacrifice required", we must agree this is true. When we look at the lives of the Major Prophets, we see men who believed in dedicated early morning worship. Before asking, they praised and reminded God of who He (God) was and what He (God) had accomplished in the past. Many times prophets would rcmind God of man's frailty, unworthiness and habitual disobedience before making their petitions known to Him.

Walk with God up to the high place.

6

Hill of Bashan

The hill of God is as the hill of Bashan; an high hill as the hill of Bashan.

Why leap ye, ye high hills? this is the hill which God desireth to dwell in; yea, the Lord will dwell in it for ever.

The chariots of God are twenty thousand, even thousands of angels: the Lord is among them, as in Sinai, in the holy place.

Thou hast ascended on high, thou hast led captivity captive: thou hast received gifts for men: yea, for the rebellious also, that the Lord God might dwell among them.

Blessed be the Lord, who daily loadeth us with benefits, even the God of our salvation. Selah.

Psalm 68:15-19 (KJV)

To come through a valley and reach the ***Hill of Bashan*** is an awesome feat; the very presence of God resides in this hill with the legion of angels sent to minister to us after the journey. The greatest benefit of this hill is that God himself is hidden among the angels to minister to us in this holy place.

There is much rejoicing upon this hill; we are over comers here, victorious champions. This is a level of higher heights, this ***Hill of Bashan*** is known for its great height, and it reaches up toward heaven, clouds rest upon this hill. It is peaceful, a perfect place to rest after the journey through one of the many valleys below it. Judah (praise) resides here; this is the refreshing and strengthening hill. Benefits freely surround us on this level.

Here there is a feeling of euphoria and contentment, a "walking in the cloud" feeling. This is "The battle is over, you can shout now" mountain. Many times we leave the ***Valley of Baca*** and rest upon the ***Hill of Bashan.***

7

Hill of Hachilah

And David abode in the wilderness in strong holds, and remained in a mountain in the wilderness of Ziph. And Saul sought him every day, but God delivered him not into his hand.

And David saw that Saul was come out to seek his life: and David was in the wilderness of Ziph in a wood.

And Jonathan Saul's son arose, and went to David into the wood, and strengthened his hand in God.

And said unto him, Fear not; for the hand of Saul my father shall not find thee; and thou shalt be king over Israel, and I shall be next unto thee; and that also Saul my father knoweth.

Then they two made a covenant before the Lord; and David abode in the wood, and Jonathan went to his house.

Then came up the Ziphites to Saul to Gibeah, saying, Doth not David hide himself with us in strong holds in the wood, in the hill of Hachilah, which is on the south of Jeshimon?

I Samuel 23:14-19 (KJV)

The enemy knows where you are hiding, but they can't get to you. God had hidden David in this hill to reveal the promise, his future was unfolding and the enemy was afraid. God sent an unimagined source to reveal his destiny, the person who should be the next king, the king's own son brought words of encouragement, to tell him that the position is yours. David came through the **valley** of the shadow of death walking with God to this **hill, this high place** only to be blessed with a "word" from the mouth of the enemy's son.

David was running from Saul and may have temporarily forgotten the Samuel anointing. Being chosen from among his brothers, who seemed to be more qualified, who looked like they should have this position is one of the minor details that he had forgotten. David wasn't thinking about the things Samuel said in the past, he was in this hill to hide. But the ***Hill of Hachilah*** wasn't meant to be just a hiding place, but also a holding place to renew the vision and reaffirm the true destiny for the chosen one.

It was in this high place that David in fear wrote Psalm 54:

Save me, o God, by thy name and judge me by thy strength.

Hear my prayer, O God; give ear to the words of my mouth.

For strangers are risen up against me, and oppressors seek after my soul: they have not set God before them. Selah

Behold, God is mine helper: the Lord is with them that uphold my soul.

He shall reward evil unto mine enemies: cut them off in thy truth.

I will freely sacrifice unto thee: I will praise thy name, O Lord; for it is good.

For he hath delivered me out of all trouble: and mine eye hath seen his desire upon mine enemies. (KJV)

It sounds as if this high place refreshed and reaffirmed the promise. David soon after moved to his next destination. When the enemy returned he was no longer in this hill, but had fled to the wilderness on the opposite side of the mountain surrounded by Saul's army. God interceded when the enemy was about to take David. Messengers summoned Saul to return home for the Philistines (Saul's enemies) had invaded his home land. This allowed David and his men to escape yet again.

The Psalm of David was answered by the actions of God. That's a benefit of this hill.

You walked out of a valley with God to be blessed by someone who should be an enemy. You walked through the valley with God and now this is the revelation: you are about to be blessed and your enemy cannot stop what God has started. Walked out to enter this high place of revelation, where destiny is revealed and affirmation renews. We learn that the enemy, the one who is chasing after us, the one who is trying to destroy us has knowledge that you are about to be blessed with his (the enemy's) blessing. You are about to walk into palaces not inherited from an earthly father, to live in houses you didn't build and partake of vineyards you didn't plant. Walk in Psalm 54 when you leave this hill being confident that God has moved the enemy.

8

Mount Carmel

And it came to pass, when Ahab saw Elijah, that Ahab said unto him, Art thou he that troubleth Israel?

And he answered, I have not troubled Israel: but thou, and thy father's house, in that ye have forsaken the commandments of the Lord, and thou hast followed Baalim.

Now therefore send, and gather to me all Israel unto mount Carmel, and the prophets of Baal four hundred and fifty, and the prophets of the groves four hundred, which eat at Jezebel's table.

So Ahab sent unto all the children of Israel, and gathered the prophets together unto mount Carmel.

And Elijah came unto all the people, and said, How long halt ye between two opinions? If the Lord be God, follow him: but if Baal, then follow him. And the people answered him not a word.

Then said Elijah unto the people, I even I only, remain a prophet of the Lord; but Baal's prophets are four hundred and fifty men.

Let them therefore give us two bullocks; and let them choose one bullock for themselves, and cut it in pieces, and lay it on wood, and put no fire under; and I will dress the other bullock, and lay it on wood, and put no fire under.

And call ye on the name of your gods, and I will call on the name of the Lord: and the God that answereth by fire, let him be God. And all the people answered and said, It is well spoken.

I Kings 18:17-24 (KJV)

So you think you are all alone, it seems that everybody else has turned back. Somewhere between the last *valley* and reaching **Mount Carmel**, this high place some have turned back, others have joined the opposition or just given up for lack of courage.

Mount Carmel will prove who you are and more importantly who God is. This is the showdown between the higher powers, your fear has left and suddenly the numbers you saw in the *valley* don't matter. "He that is for us is more than the world against us" is this mountains slogan.

It is at this high place that you just decide you have had enough. I am not running anymore, I am not hiding anymore, and I am calling you out. Elijah called the enemy to meet in his (Elijah's) high place on his (Elijah's) terms. The rules were decided by God and the challenge issued by Elijah.

It was on a mountain that Elijah challenged the prophets of Jezebel and took back the high place with a show of fire. A God sent fire that licked up water, ate dirt (dust), and repossessed God's property that had been used by the prophets of Baal for evil.

The prophets of Baal were embarrassed, confused and destroyed in this high place. The God Jehovah showed His mighty power and His redemptive authority. There is no need for Elijah to hide or fear for his life anymore. God, the Great I Am was present and answered by fire. He showed up and proved Himself omnipotent and superior to the gods made by hand.

This is your highest level, there have been other miracles and blessing on your journey through many valleys, but nothing you have been through can compare to what is about to happen. God will answer by fire and the false accusers and prophets will cease. Confirmation takes place on Mt. Carmel. All these things were very important events but something was still not finished.

There was still a ***drought,*** no moisture; everything was dry and dying or dead. God has proven Himself in this high place, and now the refreshing blessings must come, through the **RAIN.** All the other events were leading up to the rain, which is why this ***Mount Carmel, this High Place*** was created and taken back by force to release the rain. To release the things that had been held up, God had to destroy some people, move hindrances, destroy some carnal thoughts and re-establish His territory. The high place was placed back into the righteous hands of the only true God, and now the rain.

The Importance of Rain

There can be no fruit, no production without the rain.

> *But the land, whither ye go to possess it, is a land of hills and valleys, and drinketh water of the rain of heaven:*
>
> *A land which the Lord thy God careth for: the eyes of the Lord are always upon it, from the beginning of the year even unto the end of the year.*
>
> *And it shall come to pass, if ye shall hearken diligently unto my commandments which I command you this day, to love your God, and to serve him with all your heart and with all your soul,*

That I will give you the rain of your land in his due season, the first rain and the latter rain, that thou mayest gather in thy corn, and thy wine, and thine oil.

And I will send grass in thy fields for thy cattle, that thou mayest eat and be full.

Take heed to yourselves, that your heart be not deceived, and ye turn aside, and serve other gods, and worship them;

And then the Lord's wrath be kindled against you, and he shut up the heaven, that there be no rain, and that the land yield not her fruit; and lest ye perish quickly from off the good land which the Lord giveth you.

Deuteronomy 11:11-17(KJV)

Rain or moisture is necessary for producing fruit, both the first rain and the latter rain. The moisture of the rain creates growth and plays a part in the continuity of growth. Joseph became a fruitful bough that grew out of his boundaries to the high place of the wall. The rain is necessary to the reproductive processes in their renewal season. Each spring season, trees and greenery depend on the rain to bring forth fruit. Spiritually, the rain causes reaction and reproduction, we become fruitful. Ministries are birthed, books are written, bodies are healed, and broken relationships are mended because of the rain. The rain fills the pool in the valley of Baca. God hears us when we cry in the valley or tears, in our weakened, lowest state.

> *When the poor and needy seek water, and there is none, and their tongue faileth for thirst, I the Lord will hear them, I the God of Israel will not forsake them.*
> *I will open rivers in high places, and fountains in the midst of the valleys: I will make the wilderness a pool of water, and the dry land springs of water.*
> *Isaiah 41:17-18 (KJV)*

The impotent man had no one to put him into the pool at the troubling of the water. He was pushed aside, stepped over and probably stepped on by others who progressed to the healing waters. He was in the valley (right vicinity) but couldn't get to the pool (to his destiny). The pool has been filled with rain from heaven. In this valley, **"Wilt thou be made whole?** Then get up and pick up your thing that you have been hindered in and carry it out of this valley. God says, "Meet me in the high place". Jesus met the man next in the temple, the high place for further instructions.

It is when we fail in the valley experience that God withholds the rain. Through disbelief and doubt, anger, disobedience or a spirit of retaliation; the brook, the well, the pool and even the rivers of living water will dry up. We read **Deuteronomy**

28:1-15 (KJV) for the blessings God promises, but we fail to continue reading about the punishments for disobedience in the valley experience. We enter to pass through and come out better. But by our decisions there can be destruction and setbacks. The rain can change into something useless.

> *The Lord shall make the rain of thy land powder and dust: from heaven shall it come down upon thee, until thou be destroyed.*
>
> *Deuteronomy 28:24 (KJV)*

When you worship on Mount Carmel, you leave with blessings raining down upon you.

9

Mount Ararat

Genesis 8:4 (KJV) And the ark rested in the seventh month, on the seventeenth day of the month, upon the mountains of Ararat.

9:13 I do set my bow in the cloud, and it shall be for a token of a covenant between me and the earth.

And it shall come to pass, when I bring a cloud over the earth, that the bow shall be seen in the cloud:

And I will remember my covenant, which is between me and you and every living creature of all flesh; and the waters shall no more become a flood to destroy all flesh.

And the bow shall be in the cloud; and I will look upon it, that I may remember the everlasting covenant between God and every living creature of all flesh that is upon the earth.

When Noah's ark landed, it was in the high place of Mount Ararat that God made a renewed covenant with man. God used the high places as a meeting site with his deliverers and prophets. These mountainous areas were close to heaven, uninhabited by man, a quiet place, a place of solitude and worthy of a sweet communion with the almighty God. The presence of God dwells in the high places yesterday, today and forever. It was there that Moses hid in the cleft of a rock while the presence or Glory of God passed by. When Jesus was transfigured, it was on a mountain.

Mount Ararat ended a long journey and hosted the ark that carried all that was left of creation, two by two both male and female along with their offspring. The earth was destroyed by water but the seed remained. A great loss had occurred but also a new beginning. It is while resting on Ararat that the spiritual seed buds and new life begins.

This mountain represents a new beginning after a devastating loss. Noah and his family even the animals left familiar acquaintances and places behind to start afresh.

Mount Ararat represents a new beginning for the so-called losers, who turn out to be the true winners after all. Favor rests upon the shoulders of the few yet faithful inhabitants of Ararat, those who continue to build their arks because faithful God said it would rain. And in return He (God) places rainbows in the post cloudy, after the rain sky as a symbol of hope and covenant.

10

Mount Hermon

Psalm 133:3 (KJV)

When you come to this mountain, you should
expect a **"blessing"**. Dew is strange. Of all God's
creation and inventions for mankind, dew is
strange. It silently and faithfully comes every night
without fanfare or announcement. It's never talked
about or reported on the evening news, you never
know if it was heavy or light, it actually seems
unimportant. It is never preceded by thunder or
lightening, the clouds don't darken to signal its
arrival. It doesn't cause flooding or get honorable
mention in statistical data used by meteorologist,
yet it has great importance.

Have you ever thought about the faithfulness of dew? Even in drought conditions, the grass is wet every morning with this rich moisture. I can't remember a morning that it was not performing its duty. Even on cold mornings the dew presents itself as white frost.

Let's take a closer look at the dew. The **(World Book Dictionary, 1983):**

- Dew – 1. Moisture that condenses from the air and collects in small drops on cool surfaces during the night. 2. Moisture in small drops on a surface such as tears or perspiration.

- Frost – Moisture frozen on or in a surface, feathery crystals of ice formed when water vapor in the air condenses at a temperature below freezing; white frost

- Tear – 3. A bead of liquid condensed on anything
  Thou tellest my wanderings: put thou my tears into thy bottle: are they not in thy book? When I cry unto thee, then shall mine enemies turn back: this I know; for God is for me.

  Psalm 56:8, 9 (KJV)

- When we Cry - Tears – God puts them in a Bottle – then He Pours Out…Blessings – The Dew falls – as Moisture or Frost – and represent Benefits – Daily Benefits poured out upon the earth. They all three fall and affect change

There Is Something Strange About the Dew

When the Children of Israel complained about no bread to eat, the bread rationed by God came with the dew, as the dew. The blessing came with the morning dew consistently and faithfully.

When Gideon asked God for a sign, it was the dew that validated the prophecy. We can call the dew obedient and in control, as it allowed the fleece to become wet and the ground around it dry one morning and the next morning the ground to become wet and the fleece dry by Gideon's request.

This mountain is rich because of the dew. The soil is rich and conducive to the growing process because of the moisture. Dew is gentle, refreshing and pure.

Mount Hermon is the high place of gentle refreshing. We walk upon this high place to receive, it is host to an early morning blessed walk. Promises along with grace, mercy and favor are new every morning; it is one of the most peaceful places of anointing. *Mount Hermon* is the place for morning praise and worshippers.

There is a secret to early morning walks upon *Hermon*. The birds are aware of hidden secrets, small blessings that fall each night with the dew drops. They quietly gather goodies from the grass and sing their loudest at this early morning feast, as if to give praise to God.

Each morning God's mercies are renewed; it is clear to God's chosen vessels that early meetings with our father yield the greatest benefits that are daily gifted to us. The high places are filled with His presence early and spiritual things are released from heaven to descend down, as the dew first to the high places and then to the earth. Those who seek early in the high places reap rewards for getting up from a rested state to meet God.

There is a refreshing both spiritually and naturally early in the morning on Mount Hermon. During the night the body goes through a process of renewal and by morning has revived itself to start afresh. We awake with the dried secretions around our eyes, evidence that some cleansing took place during the resting state. There are pieces of hair and flakes of dead skin cells that may not be seen by the naked eye, but a microscope of the resting place would reveal many hidden secrets that our body shed during the night. There are things that have come off of us during the night to prepare the body for a new day. We yawn; we stretch and sigh to release and to receive.

Every great prophet, priest and successful person of God started early and high. There were physical hills and groves just for worship. So in the twenty-first century, we ask, "Where is the high place?" The mountains are far away from our homes, the hills have been reduced to paved concrete, and the groves have become landscape or excavated for suburbia. Where is the high place?

At three A.M. the high place is either the living room floor, or at four A.M. it's the garage or the basement, or at five A.M. it's the bedroom floor, or the balcony of our upstairs apartment. It has become crucial that we re-create a high place in the twenty first century. Because we don't see a physical hill or grove, there are some who may feel this is not necessary. But according to God's word, there is "spiritual wickedness in high places". The battles we fight are not with flesh and blood, there are greater forces behind the faces and looks. And the harsh words that cut through to the heart and soul. Wicked forces are in the high places, height creates advantage in any war. If we are to be victorious we must retake the hill. Strategic warfare is in order; those who meet early control the high places.

When we get "just one more hour" of sleep, we lose "just one more hour" of communion with God. He faithfully wakes us on time for early morning communion and we reach for the "snooze" temptation. There is a difference between sleep and snooze to the early morning high place worshipper. When God wakes us there are things that alert the body to morning and mental things begin to take place. But when we try to return to the sleep state, problems arise, because snooze does not allow enough time for the body to reach REM again. There is confusion as to time and other forces have taken the high place. The second awaking becomes frustration and rushing to meet the demands of the day, everything is thrown out of sequence, bottom line you have lost the hill.

There are now other forces controlling your day. Have to go back into the house to get your glasses or a report that is due today, slow traffic or wreck on the drive to work, you take an alternate route only to run into another accident. The whole day is filled with mishaps and frustration. Snooze is not good.

When a soldier is awakened in the early dawn by the drill sergeant or commanding officer's voice, there is no snooze button. In fact there are no other options except to get up and start the day. The rules are set, the schedule is non-negotiable. Get up at the sound of my voice, get into formation, and perform the ritual we have established for our day. It is the same as the day before; there is no deviating from the plan.

God's plan is that we give him our "early" while the dew rests upon Mount Hermon, our high place. When we are dedicated to the high place gathering, waking up gets easier. The first few times the alarm clock may help us to remember that it is time for prayer. If you live near a farm, there is no doubt a faithful rooster will start the day with a timely crow. Just as he did for Peter, the rooster (cock) serves as a reminder of one prediction fulfilled and one promise broken.

Why did Jesus base his prediction to Peter on a rooster? Because he knew that early in the morning without fail, the rooster would climb to a high place and crow. This was a predictable act by one of God's creations. We all should have the mind of a rooster; I'll get up early and climb to my high place to do what I do best. Some believe the rooster crows to show his dominance, to mark his territory. His dedication to being the first one up and making "noise" that is distinctly his own proves a point and all predators know there is a protector of the family on his post early. It is awesome when the husband like the rooster, takes the lead position as God intended. The rooster doesn't have an alarm clock; he naturally wakes up to go to the high place early to crow.

Getting to Mount Hermon early should be a ritual that receives new revelation along with the new mercies of God daily. The prayers and praises we give should not become ritualistic, but the act of getting up to the high place early should become natural. Abraham didn't think twice about getting to the high place early, it became natural to him as a part of his day, the prayers were not always the same and the instructions were never the same. If mercies are new every morning, so are the revelations and therefore our requests and adorations should reflect the newness of the day. Naturally we can say I love you to the same person every day, but there must be new ways of showing that affection. The saying, "actions speak louder than words", is true for our Jehovah. It may be that all He wants us to do on one of those early mornings is just listen to the instructions.

When Moses went up to the high place to receive the Ten Commandments, he had to listen and not make requests in the middle of the conversation. God was doing an awesome work and only needed Moses attention to the details He was giving him, just listen to the instructions.

Every test experienced at the hands of Pharaoh prepared Moses for this high place encounter. Moses learned the voice of God in those trying times, from the first burning bush meeting to the mountaintop delivery of the Ten Commandments. He learned to trust the voice of God and to believe that there is always a way out of the valley, out of every situation.

Just as the eagle stirs the nest and allows the thorns to make it uncomfortable for the eaglets, so God sends an uncomfortable thing to move us out of the valley. It's not meant to be a dwelling place but a place to pass through. The thorn stimulates and causes movement out of familiar surroundings. You'll never begin the climb up and out as long as you feel surrounded and safe. The eagle stirs the nest but it's up to the eaglet to climb up to the edge of the nest and prepare for flight, despite the fear and uncertainty. Daddy eagle circles around waiting on the fall, ensuring a rescuer is available.

The winds are favorable; conditions have been met for the journey.

> *He found him in a desert land, and in the waste howling wilderness; he led him about, he instructed him, as the apple of his eye.*
>
> *As an eagle stirreth up her nest, fluttereth over her young, spreadeth abroad her wings, taketh them, beareth them on her wings:*
>
> *So the Lord alone did lead him, and there was no strange god with him.*
>
> *Deuteronomy 32:10-12 (KJV)*

11

Mount Peor

Numbers 23:28 (KJV) And Balak brought Baalam unto the top of Peor, That looketh toward Jeshimon.

24:10 And Balak's anger was kindled against Baalam, and he smote his hands together: and Balak said unto Baalam, I called thee to curse mine enemies, and, behold, thou hast altogether blessed them these three times.

Therefore now flee thou to thy place: I thought to promote thee unto great honour; but lo, the Lord hath kept thee back from honour.

This high place, **Mount Peor,** is inhabited by your enemies to curse you while you are in your valley, minding your own business. It was necessary to include this high place because instead of a curse, it really is a blessing to us. We walk beneath and are yet blessed.

The Children of Israel were in the valley beneath Mount Peor, going about their business enjoying the Lord unaware that Baalam and Balak were in this high place plotting and scheming to destroy them. Someone in the Israelite camp was living holy; someone was under God's covering while the enemy physically inhabited this mountain.

God reigns over **Mount Peor.** Three times Balaam attempted to curse and three times God blessed. The enemy will use your mountain to try and overthrow the blessings of your heritage or take your inheritance, but there is a place in God called **covered.** Where the forces of heaven will not allow any bad thing to happen, nor withhold any good thing. Even the enemy's curses changed to blessings will be honored on this mountain. What the devil meant for evil in your fruitful season, God turned it around.

When we are chosen by God, everything works for our good. Our bad experiences become a testimony for a weaker person who crosses our path. Our victory becomes our strength in future battles. We can't tell the eaglet to face the sun and fly directly into it, if we haven't taken the journey ourselves.

Let the enemy curse you on this mountain if he dares. When he (the enemy) finishes his so-called curse, your blessings begin. Living under the shadow of *Mount Peor*, the Promise, the Covenant and the Favor of God grants prestige and covering in challenging times. Dangers seen and unseen are covered under your policy.

For every tear, God sends provision and blessings. Joseph went through *Baca*, while the enemy cursed him on *Mount Peor.* But he didn't leave empty-handed. He was called a fruitful bough by *a well.* ***"Who passing through the valley of Baca make it a well".*** We need the tears to make the well to produce the fruit.

A well is a reservoir; it holds the excess or overflow until it is needed. But first the well must be created or dug out to prepare for what is expected and then the water comes. Wells produce water which is very important for the preservation of life. The flocks drank from the well and food production required a well.

There are times when you know the enemy is watching from *Peor* but you just keep digging the well anyway. Abraham dug a well that was violently taken away from him by the enemies of his *Mount Peor.* He didn't get angry and fight in his *valley*, instead he blessed his enemy. The well was restored and Abraham then created a grove of worship, a high place.

With her tears coming up before God, she was told to stop being afraid, God has already heard the child's voice and prepared a well of water to save his life. Walking through the ***Valley of Baca***, God will prepare a well with our tears, and fill the pool with heaven's rain.

There is no greater example of Baca (tears) than the story of Job and his sufferings. After losing his children, his livelihood and worldly possessions, his wife added insult to injury. "Curse God, and die". These words catapulted Job into a deeper depression, but he did not sin with his lips. With each catastrophe, Job went deeper into the Valley of Baca. Passing through he began to make it a well, it became a fruitful place, and it brought him to a place of trust in Jehovah. It's at the point of reaching our limits, our dead end that we remember God. There's a point in time, while passing through Baca that we realize we have cried enough, repented enough and searched our hearts enough. We are broken and at this point our crying can turn into wailing. Tears lead us to the high place to worship God, from the valley of Baca to the high place. The valley is the lowest point and we can only climb up to the high place.

> *My face is foul with weeping, and on*
> *my eyelids is the shadow of death:*
> *Not for any injustice in mine hands:*
> *also my prayer is pure.*
> *O earth, cover not thou my blood, and*
> *let my cry have no place.*
> *Also now, behold, my witness is in*

heaven, and my record is on high.
My friends scorn me: but mine eye poureth out tears unto God.

Job 16:16-20 (KJV)

Blessed is the man, who passing through this temporary **valley** makes it a well. It's like taking lemons and making lemonade. You know you are in this valley, crying and in pain, in need but yet blessed. Waiting beneath **Mount Peor** in a holding position, not understanding why you're spending the extra day in the shadow of this mountain. But yet trusting God, that He is faithful who promised, delay at this well is wrapped in destiny. Being productive in the **Valley of Baca**, the blessed man patiently makes a well to fill a thirst. Joseph was innocent yet trouble pursued him in his valley experience because of who he was to become. Not days but years of separation and false accusations, imprisonment, left behind after interpreting the dream, yet through all of his enduring he remained humble. He created a well in his **Valley of Baca** while the evil forces of his **Mount Peor** were cursing his destiny. God filled it (his well) with manifold blessings. In his latter end, he received a double portion. Jacob described him as, ***"a fruitful bough, even a fruitful bough by a well; whose branches run over the wall:"***

That is overflow and increase, double for your trouble in the valley experience. Joseph became fruitful and overran his boundaries; he exceeded his own expectations and the enemies' limitations. In the valley there is no understanding of our outcomes to greater levels at the high place.

After killing the Egyptian soldier, Moses fled toward the land of Midian to his valley of Baca. Guilt and shame guided him to create a well right into a greater destiny, a larger than imagined outcome. The realization was that Moses felt terrible, his actions had taken another man's life, and he was guilty of murder. Alone in this dry desert, he entered his valley of Baca. From the palace to the well to the high place where he met God at the burning bush. God already knew the plan when Moses entered the valley. Like many of us this was not a planned trip for Moses. He was driven to this valley experience out of fear and guilt. God uses difficult situations to move us out of comfort and relaxed atmospheres to a greater calling and anointing. His ultimate goal is for us to reach the higher places to gain insight and instruction for our calling. Other people depended on Moses journey into his personal valley of Baca. Whether it's to write a book, start a business or service others through our journey, there is a greater good that we eventually come to understand.

The Samaritan woman met Jesus sitting on a natural well that led her to a well of destiny. We learn the purpose of the well, the necessity of preparing a well in Baca to receive the overflowing waters. It was here that He offered living water to quench an otherwise unquenchable thirst.

"...*the water that I shall give him shall be in him a well of water springing up into everlasting life.*"

From the valley of shame to the well she created to the high place, she ran through the city crying, ***"Come see a man"***. Many were affected, delivered and even saved by this woman's journey into Baca. She was a sinner that created a well to receive. In our filthy, sinful state God sees into our future. Saul persecuted the saints, but how effective a witness he became as Paul after entering the valley of Baca. We enter one way and exit with name changes, new personalities, fresh starts, clear consciences, clean slates, renewed minds, delivered souls, clarity of visions, burdens lifted, forgiveness, new attitudes, restored joy, full of glory and power. Demons recognize who we are as we leave this valley and enter the high places. The valley is simply a low place.

Jesus fasted forty days and became hungry in the low place. He then entered the high place to be tempted. If Satan had known that this was the place the valley was preparing Jesus for, he would not have suggested escorting Jesus to this higher place. It was here that Jesus reclaimed what Satan thought that he himself owned. He went from the pinnacle of the temple in the "holy city" to an "exceeding high mountain" to offer Christ things that were no longer his to give. He no longer had possession of this domain.

> *They that sow in tears shall reap in joy. He that goeth forth and weepeth, bearing precious seed shall doubtless come again with rejoicing, bringing his sheaves with him.*
>
> *Psalm 126:5, 6*

Joseph didn't leave empty-handed, in fact when Israel blessed his sons, Joseph was given a double portion. There's a saying, "double for your trouble", he had two sons who were blessed by their grandfather, Israel. When God blesses us we don't even have to fight, the wealth of the wicked becomes our inheritance for the tears. Before Israel died he blessed his sons and Joseph received the greater blessing.

> *Moreover I have given to thee one portion above thy brethren, which I took out of the hand of the Amorite with my sword and with my bow.*
>
> *Genesis 48:22*

You don't have to fight, just cry. You are promised an inheritance; God does not allow us to leave the valley empty-handed. We are not the heirs of the inheritance, but because we passed through Baca, we are entitled to the same benefits. The scripture calls us strangers or aliens, but we get an inheritance, *because* we have been through Baca.

> *And it shall come to pass, that ye shall divide it by lot for an inheritance unto you, and to the strangers that sojourn among you, which shall begat children among you: and they shall be unto you as born in the country among the children of Israel; they shall have inheritance with you among the tribes of Israel.*
>
> *And it shall come to pass, that in what tribe the stranger sojourneth, there shall ye give him his inheritance, saith the Lord God.*
>
> *Ezekiel 47:22, 23*

David cut off the head of Goliath and brought it to King Saul. The children of Israel didn't leave Egypt empty, they carried away gold and silver, expensive clothes and shoes of their enemies. They didn't steal even an earring, they simply asked for them.

When God fights the battle, the spoils belong to you. God promised Abram (Abraham), your seed will be a stranger and servant in a foreign land; they will be afflicted for four hundred years. But when they come out, they will have great substance. Our battles may not always seem easy but God sets us up to be blessed.

12

Mount of Olives

Matthew 24;3 And as he sat upon the mount of Olives, the disciples came unto him privately, saying, Tell us when shall these things be? And what shall be the sign of thy coming, and of the end of the world?

And Jesus answered and said unto them, Take heed that no man deceive you.

For many shall come in my name, saying I am Christ, and shall deceive many.

And ye shall hear of wars and rumors of wars: see that ye be not troubled: for all these things must come to pass, but the end is not yet.

For nation shall rise against nation, and kingdom against kingdom: and there shall be famines and pestilences, and earthquakes, in divers places.

All these are the beginning of sorrows.

Then shall they deliver you up to be afflicted, and shall kill you: and ye shall be hated of all nations for my name's sake.

And then shall many be offended, and shall be betray one another, and shall hate one another.

And many false prophets shall rise, and shall deceive many.

And because iniquity shall abound, the love of many shall wax cold.

But he that shall endure unto the end, the same shall be saved.

And this gospel of the kingdom shall be preached in all the world for a witness unto all nations, and then shall the end come.

Receive the word of the Lord. The **Mount of Olives** holds prophecy, warnings and revelation. Jesus sermon was not hard to understand but He used parables to help convey the message of **Judgment. I would call this a *Mountain of Preparation.*** Will you be ready?

On this mountain, there is an opportunity to search the heart, spirit and soul to see if there is oil in the lamp. The righteous *scarcely* make in (to the kingdom of God [Heaven]). **The Mount of Olives** prophecies that even with all our good deeds and almsgiving there are some who will not enter the kingdom of God. There will be prophets, preachers, evangelist and apostles in hell. There will be people with good works who have no oil in their vessels.

We walk in our sins until a disaster comes and reminds us that we are sinners saved by grace. When a natural disaster disrupts our normal activities, we form prayer groups and fasting ideas out of fear. How quickly we forget when the television news stops reporting and the conversation is no longer a hot topic in the breakroom.

On this mountain Jesus gave us the parable (earthly story with a heavenly meaning) of the fig tree, the ten virgins, and the talents.

The Fig Tree

- *Belongs to the mulberry family of trees, a group of strong trees*
- *One of the last trees to produce its leaves and fruit before summer*
- *It is a sure signal that summer is near*
- *Represents the signs of the times, after the fulfillment of the prophecy, when everything else has bloomed, the Lord will make His entrance*

The Talents

- *What are you doing with God's stuff, the talents that He left in your hand?*

- *The talents were given without instructions. Its left up to you what to do with the gifts He entrusted to you*
- *Those who gained had to make contact with others who were productive in order to gain other talents*
- *If you put your talent in the ground (hide it), it becomes of no use. No one benefits from your hidden talent.*

The Ten Virgins

- *Five were wise-they took extra oil, preparing for the unexpected. Knew their purpose was to meet the bridegroom at any time day or night.*
- *Five were foolish-depended on one source, what they already had in the lamp. Unprepared for the darkness.*
- *Most marriages are held in the daytime, God is not NORMAL*

In this twenty-first century, we need to re-visit the **Mount of Olives.** These parables are just as important now as when Jesus spoke the words out of His mouth. Will you be ready?

13

Mount Calvary

And when they were come to the place, which is called Calvary, there they crucified him, and the malefactors, one on he right hand, and the other on the left.

Luke 23:33 (KJV)

Crucify the flesh daily. The spirit needs to be released in this high place before the Glory of the Lord can enter. **Mount Calvary** is our place of transition into usefulness, from brokenness into spirituality. We must die to fleshly sin into victorious, eternal life.

After the crucifixion, Christ released bound souls, set captives free and took the vital keys from the hands of the enemy. We have that same authority when we visit **Mount Calvary**.

When we deny this flesh and seek the more of God, we become instruments of change. The atmosphere changes, people around us change, situations change, things begin to move forward to the next level. After Jesus crucifixion, the demons and devils were quiet. After death Christ became stronger, it was not the ending but the beginning again, the rebirth into the role of Savior and Intercessor sitting on the right hand of the Father. There are some things that couldn't happen until the crucifixion.

It took the blood of the last sacrificial lamb, Jesus Christ, to atone for the sins of mankind. The blood of bulls, sheep and other innocent animals were losing their effectiveness with God. The odor that was once a sweet smell in his nostrils now sickened him. Man continually offered animal sacrifices and yet sinned over and over again. There seemed to be no remission of sin. No man or animal on earth could do this task; it called for unimaginable strength and commitment. The character of the Savior would be tested many times before the crucifixion; humbleness, gentleness, compassion and genuine love were needed by the chosen vessel to carry out God's plan of salvation.

The blood flowing through his veins looked like human blood but there was a difference that mere eyes and microscopes could not detect.

There are things that can't be birthed out or prophetically released until we reach **Calvary.** We want the glory but not the crucifixion, we want the popularity and notoriety, but not the suffering associated with crucifixion. There is blood loss, dehydration, pain, agonizing pain, brief loss of consciousness, and confusion in the process of crucifixion dying. But the wake up is a weightless soaring to new heights, a transfiguration on the mountain with heavenly recognition.

Mount Calvary is your mountain of transformation into useable material. The mind is transformed and renewed, there is a greater anointing. The spiritual man will never be the old human man again.

When they seek you early, you will already be up doing your work, for greater works are in you when you leave ***Calvary's mountain.***

14

Mount Nebo

Get thee up into this mountain Abarim, unto mount Nebo, which is in the land of Moab, that is over against Jericho; and behold the land of Canaan, which I give unto the children of Israel for a possession.

Deuteronomy 32:49 (KJV)

Let's view the Promised Land from our **Mount Nebo.** There have been many times that we have gone from valley to valley victoriously on a promise. We encouraged ourselves because we knew that there was something awaiting us for our perseverance and faithfulness. The Lord allows us to see the end result, to view the prize, a possession that only existed in our thoughts and dreams until we entered **Mount Nebo.**

God takes us up high to see what the hunger and thirst of our journey was taking us to possess. We went through many valleys, experienced much heartache and pain, faced death and disease, famine and plenty, emotional ups and downs to get to this place. The beauty of this peek into the future is filled with "shock and awe" that goes beyond what we could have ever imagined in our minute minds. We didn't think big enough, nor large enough to explain what we are about to walk into. This is an enlarged territory that we view from *Mount Nebo.*

From *Mount Nebo,* we can see ourselves in the future and we look better spiritually. We have been transformed from a child to an adult, from a Gentile sinner saved by grace to an over-comer walking in favor with God and man. There are visions of victories dancing in our heads, we can see the walls of Jericho falling, enemies fleeing before us in defeat, and giants are falling. We see ourselves running through troops and leaping over walls, wearing the armor of God – the helmet of salvation, the breastplate of rightcousness, our feet are shod with the preparation of the gospel, and we have the shield of faith. The sword we carry is sharp; the weapons of this warfare are not carnal but spiritual. This is not a war of flesh and blood; we did that in the valleys in our human bodies. But *Mount Nebo* shows a different picture.

15

Mount Zion

But in the last day it shall come to pass, that the mountain of the house of the Lord shall be established in the top of the mountains, and it shall be exalted above the hills; and people shall flow unto it.

And many nations shall come, and say, Come, and let us go up to the mountain of the Lord, and to the house of the God of Jacob; and he will teach us of his ways, and we will walk in his paths: for the law shall go forth of Zion, and the word of the Lord from Jerusalem.

Micah 4:1-2 (KJV)

Blow ye the trumpet in Zion, and sound the alarm in my holy mountain: let all the inhabitants of the land tremble: for the day of the Lord cometh, for it is nigh at hand:

And it shall come to pass, that whosoever shall call on the name of the Lord shall be delivered: for in mount Zion and in Jerusalem shall be deliverance, as the Lord hath said, and in the remnant whom the Lord shall call.

Joel 2:1, 32 (KJV)

Mount Zion-Heaven.

One of the first mentions of heaven is in Genesis 28:12, the dream of Jacob's ladder. A ladder that reached to heaven and the angels of God were ascending and descending on it. And in the dream, God stood above the ladder identifying himself as the God of Abraham and Isaac. This served as a reminder to Jacob of past promises made by God to his ancestors.

The ascending and descending angels served as messengers between heaven and earth. They were transporters of words, promises, visions, and manifestations to earthly recipients. Whenever we think of heaven, terms such as beautiful, peaceful, rewarding, streets of gold, mansions, crowns and a royal robe enter our thoughts. One wise person declared that heaven is a prepared place for a prepared people. Heaven is a promise of all promises to the believers who daily endure hardness to enter in and receive their heavenly riches.

The earthly Mount Zion is a hill located in Jerusalem; and upon this hill stood the temple of worship. The presence of God rests in Zion. Many have looked toward Mount Zion for answers to hopeless situations. This holy hill is a pavilion, a high tower, a fortress in times of trouble; a place or security. And more than these it is a hill of worship, a high place of covenant where the presence of God dwells. Early the Lord visits this hill to commune with true committed worshippers, who set aside the dawn religiously to praise Jehovah. While the early morning dew rests upon this high place, they without fail rise early and command the atmosphere to be at peace; strongholds are removed, territories are taken by force in Mount Zion.

To Joel and Micah God revealed the finality of promises and covenant agreements. The day of the Lord is coming, "blow the trumpet, sound the alarm" in this high place.

God, Jehovah is seeking believers who are unafraid to enter the high places and declare the true and living God reigns. The high places of Baal (Spiritual Wickedness) must be taken by force and reclaimed as on Mount Carmel. After reclaiming Mount Carmel, God relieved the famine by sending much needed rain. There is a movement in the earth and wailing, travailing women are among the forerunners of the prophecy. God is about to send a destroying wind. He has heard the cry of a woman in travail. Women of God must travail and bring forth. During this time of pain, the cry is real and sincere. It is loud and demands attention. It stirs and moves God to open His deaf ear, His compassions stir and He reverses curses, a destroying God transforms and rethinks His decision. But often not until the destroyer has completed all or part of the task he was assigned. There are some who must be moved, some who must be destroyed before deliverance can be effective. As in the case of Jezebels prophets, destruction ensured spiritual cleansing and prosperity of the flow of the spirit. The filth and the stink were removed from the face of God on this holy ground. Hezekiah had to remove, brake, cut and destroy to ensure God's return to His people. Afterward, Hezekiah prospered and continued in the presence of God.

> *"And the Lord was with him; he prospered whithersoever he went forth."*
>
> *(II Kings18:7)*

Gideon had to destroy the altar of Baal and cut down the grove beside it, because God commanded him to do so. God cannot dwell with the unclean gods. They must be removed and destroyed before He enters back into His place of Glory. By being obedient Gideon found favor with Jehovah. He stepped out afraid but committed to obedience and proved God faithful that had promised.

If the building must be clean so must our hearts and minds be purged and circumcised. This can only be accomplished through daily devotions and repentance. To return to the high places, the conditions must be right. We cannot enter in unworthy and loaded with impurities and imperfections. Often we want to carry people who God has deemed unworthy of the call. Time is of the essence and we cry because we must leave behind flesh and blood in pursuit of the high places. Possessions must be abandoned to pursue the high places.

God sent angels to bring Lot and his family out of an imperfect place with a command to not look back, Abraham was told to leave his family behind and walk by faith toward a promise not visualized. On the way he messed up had to retreat and start again at the high place. Often God's sends us back to the place we started for clarification and to remold the plan in our mind. Distractions will come, delays are inevitable but when we come to ourselves, fear begins to mobilize instead of stagnate; anxiety begins to drive us to reclaim the high places. We become the human host that dares to snatch down the groves and high places of little gods and call back the true God's presence.

The climb from the valley floor to the surrounding mountain won't be easy for the inexperienced climber. Through many trips through

Baca and other valleys, a traveler learns that there are many ways to get through the valleys. Prayer, faith, fasting, renewal, reconnecting with God and the plan He created for us and submission to His will. Many travelers choose to climb out or fly out as eagles.

When experienced mountain climbers take on the challenge to scale a tall mountain they travel as teams, usually three to four climbers. But in the winter months, during the hardest climbs a minimum of four climbers is the rule. Shadrach, Meshach and Abednego met the requirements for a team of climbers, but they needed one more to meet the minimum requirement for four. The fourth mountain climber (fire walker) that day was the Son of God walking with them in the midst of the fire.

There are times when the Father, Son and Holy Ghost have to come in and make the climb successful. It can't be accomplished on the strength of an inexperienced climber alone.

Successful climbs from a valley are measured by your ability to reach the top of the mountain. With every attempt there is the danger of slipping back down; weather conditions may hamper ascents, requiring us to abort and start all over again. But we must have the mentality of mountain climbers; they never give up until they reach their goal.

Experienced Faith Walkers

One man who walked with God (walker) saw Him in a burning bush that was not consumed, a walker found a ram in the thicket as he in obedience was about to slay his beloved son as a sacrifice. A walker defeated hundreds of prophets of Baal in a mountainous region trusting God, another walked through the valley of the shadow of death without fear. Another received the mantel of his predecessor and led the Children of Israel into the Promised Land. One dared to walk upon the water.

We must also walk humbly through valleys, upon hills, mountains and High Places. Destiny brings us to these places that require motion to climb. Motions to glorify magnify and to worship is why we were created.

Who knows if God will answer by fire or show His hinder part, or even enable us to visualize the cloud, the size of a man's hand that holds the abundant rain of blessings? When we walk with God the vision will unfold in the walk, healing and deliverance will come, a book will be written, and an anointing will be poured out, or perhaps a revelation will be given to those chosen few. **The Least of these believed and walked by faith.**

The act of walking will generate an action from God, because He honors servants who seek the crumbs and those who would settle for a touch of his garment. The woman with the issue of blood walked toward Jesus until she couldn't walk any closer, she then had to press by faith just to touch his garment. By her actions she was healed. The centurion soldier was unworthy of the Master's attention, but by faith he came in search of a miracle. The Samaritan woman broke the rules and had a conversation with a Jew, enabling her to leave the well with everlasting water. A thief gained entry into heaven to experience an eternal walk as he hung beside his dying Savior and dared to interrupt the death of Christ with a simple plea. **Jesus walked.**

He that saith he abideth in him ought himself also so to walk, even as he walked.
I John 1:6 KJV

Heaven is our highest point, our ultimate high place. No fleshly mortal can ever dwell there. It is a prepared place for a prepared people, designated for the over-comers, the faith walkers who started to walk, then to climb and finally to conquer.

Is God pleased with your walk?

Walk with God.

"I can do all things through Christ
which strenghteneth me."

Philippians 4:13